Find out with us !

WORDS

by Karen O´Callaghan

Illustrated by

Eric Rowe and Bob Hersey

ball

fish

Brimax Books·Newmarket·England

ISBN 0 86112 174 0
All rights reserved
© Brimax Rights Ltd 1983
Published by Brimax Books
Newmarket England 1983
Second printing 1984
Printed in Belgium

Looking for words

"How can I write 'house'?"
says Zoe.
"I will turn the pages and look
for 'h'," says Alex.

Aa

Bb

alligator	ant	ambulance
apple	astronaut	airport
ball	boat	bicycle
bus	bed	bird

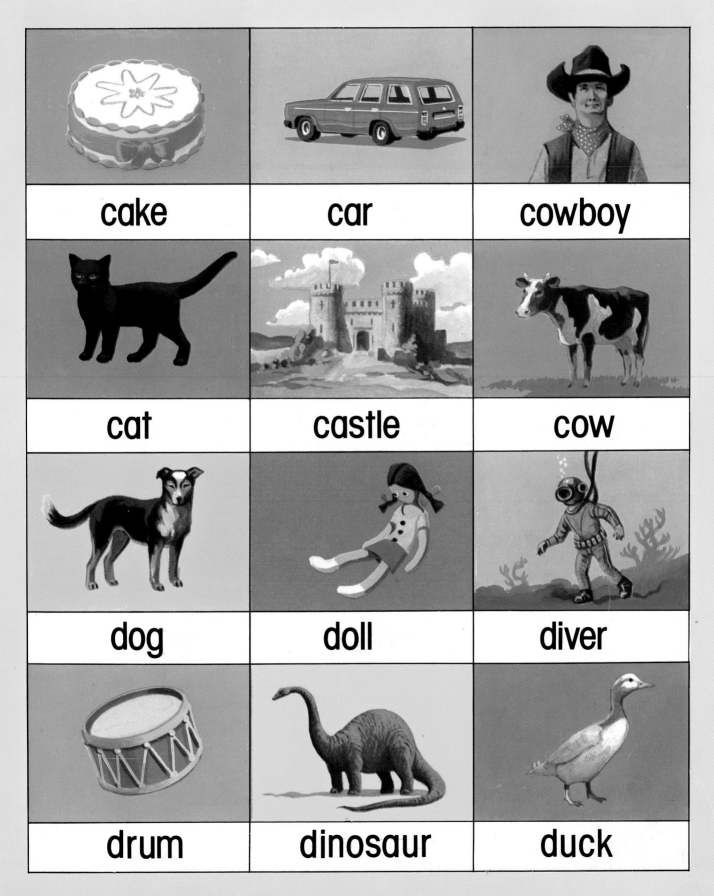

cake	car	cowboy
cat	castle	cow
dog	doll	diver
drum	dinosaur	duck

crocodile	crown	clown
crane	crab	clock
donkey	door	dress
dolphin	driver	desk

Ee   Ff

egg	elephant	eskimo
envelope	eagle	emu
fire-engine	fish	flag
flowers	fruit	frog

Gg

Hh

garage	garden	gloves
grapes	giraffe	gorilla
helicopter	house	hospital
hammer	horse	hamster

Ii

Jj

Indian	igloo	ice cream
island	insect	iron
jigsaw	jellyfish	jeans
jet plane	jaguar	jug

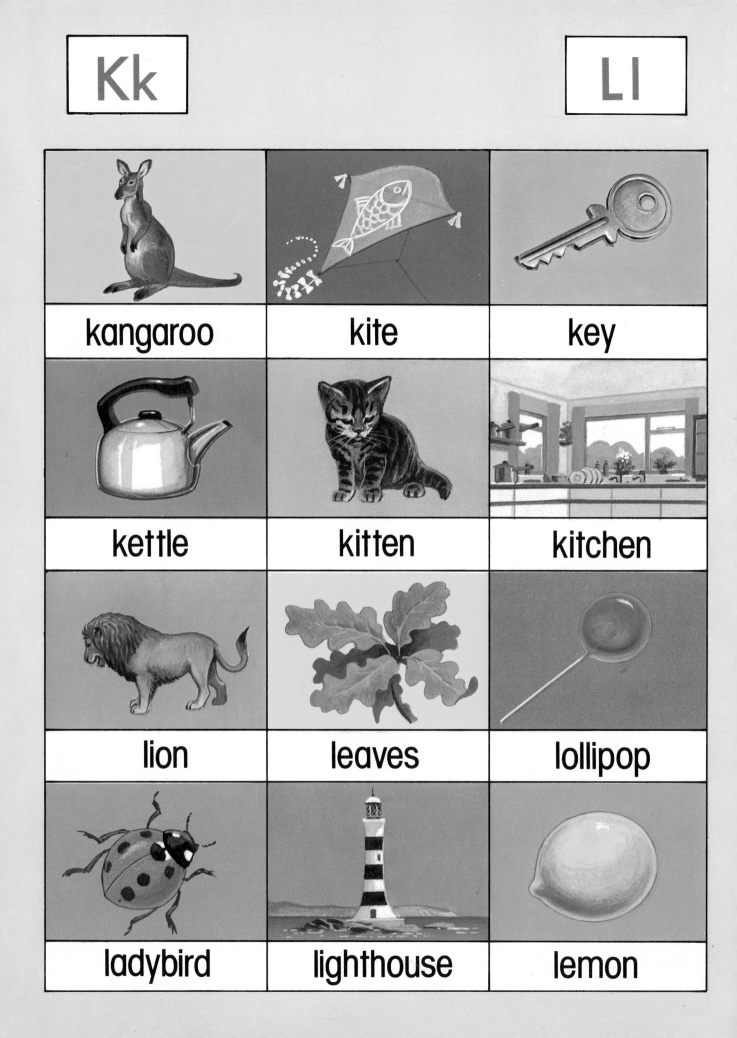

kangaroo	kite	key
kettle	kitten	kitchen
lion	leaves	lollipop
ladybird	lighthouse	lemon

Mm

Nn

moon	monkey	motorcycle
mouse	mask	milk
nest	night	nuts
newspaper	necklace	net

octopus	orange	ostrich
owl	onion	oven
pig	picnic	puppet
parachute	party	pirate

Oo **Pp**

Qq

Rr

quarter	quilt	quads
quail	quarrel	quiet
rabbit	rocket	rose
radio	robin	racing car

snake	spaceship	sun
submarine	school	shark
telephone	tree	train
television	tortoise	tiger

Uu

Vv

umbrella	unicorn	under
upside down	upstairs	umpire
visit	vegetables	volcano
violin	vulture	valentine

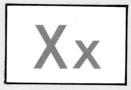

water	woods	whale
wedding	watch	wasp
x-ray	xylophone	boxer
fox	box	ox

Not many words begin with X – Here are some words with X
in the middle or at the end.

Yy   Zz

yacht	yolk	yo-yo
yawn	yak	yard
zebra	zip	zig-zag

zoo

Ways to begin to write

Here is a __ __ __ __ __

This is my __ __ __ __ __

I can see __ __ __ __ __

I went to __ __ __ __ __

First draw a picture. Choose one line on this page to begin writing.
Look for other words you need in the pages of this book.

Little words we can use

it	me	at	up
is	my	an	he
on	we	am	do
to	us	go	if

and	had	she	out
the	saw	you	new
are	his	get	fun
has	her	for	our

they	like	into	look
make	made	with	help
went	dear	love	from
some	down	said	none

Ways to start a story

Once upon a time there was_____

Long long ago there lived_____

One day_____

In the land of_____

First draw a picture. Choose one line on this page to begin your story. Look for other words you need in the pages of this book.

king	queen	prince	princess
witch	wizard	ghost	giant
dragon	fairy	mermaid	elf

More than one....

one house

two houses

girls

boys

toys

What they are like

big	little	fat	thin
old	new	hot	cold
good	wicked	happy	sad

in	out	fast	slow
thick	thin	empty	full
light	heavy	tall	short

old	young	straight	crooked
ugly	pretty	more	less
wet	dry	up	down

Making a rainbow

| red | blue | yellow | green | orange |
| purple | brown | pink | black | white |

Numbers

one	1	two	2	three	3	four	4

five	5	six	6	seven	7

eight	8	nine	9	ten	10

Our family

Zoe is my sister	Alex is my brother
Alex	Zoe

Mother	Father
Grandmother	Grandfather
Aunt	Uncle
cousins	baby

Things we can do...

We like this game.

It is fun.

We take turns to throw

the hoops at the target.

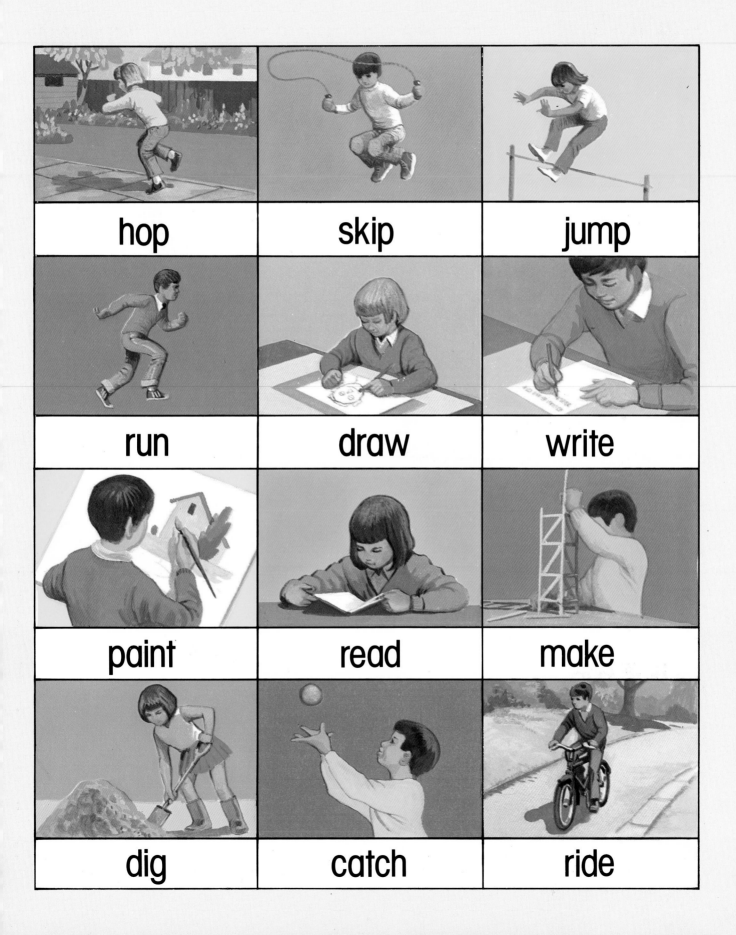

hop	skip	jump
run	draw	write
paint	read	make
dig	catch	ride

Places to go...

We like to go to the beach.

We can play on the beach

with our friends.

We can make sand castles.

zoo

park

playground

farm

library

fair

The weather

Looking out of the window.

We can see it is raining.

The water drips and splashes.

It makes puddles.

snowing

foggy

sunny

windy

frosty

stormy

People we know

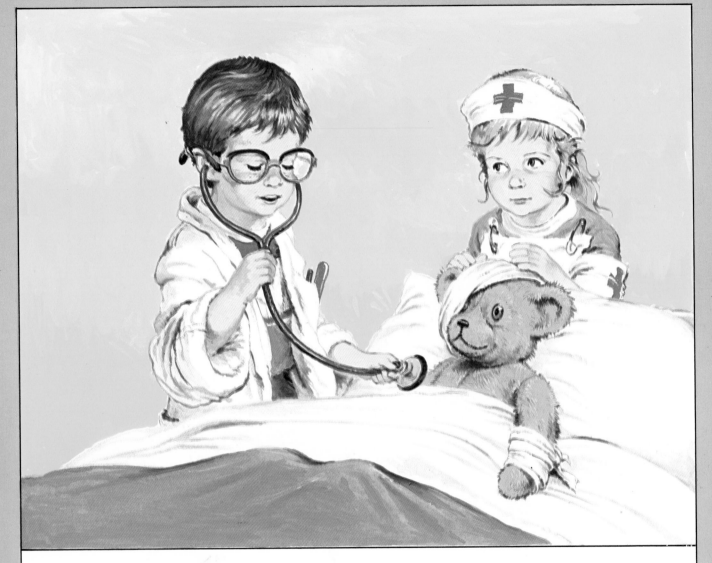

We can play a game.

Alex is the doctor.

Zoe is the nurse.

Teddy is ill. We can make him better.

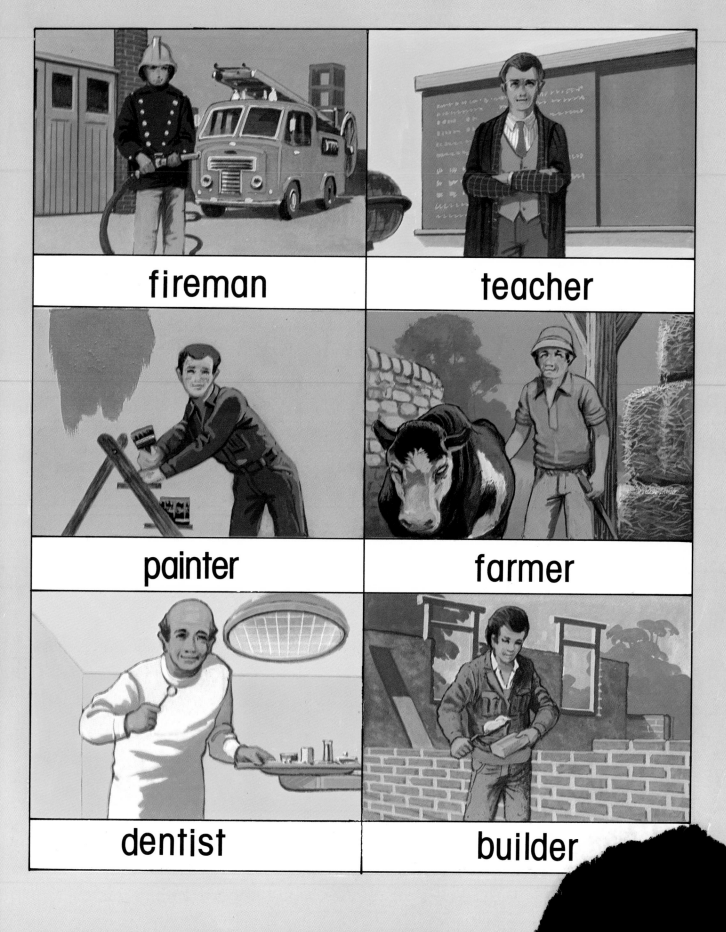

fireman

teacher

painter

farmer

dentist

builder

Which day is it?

Yesterday was Sunday

Today is Monday

Tomorrow will be Tuesday

Wednesday

Thursday

Friday

Saturday

ning   afternoon   evening

In one day we....

get up	wash	dress
eat	work	play
watch	undress	bath
listen	go to bed	sleep

This is my ball

The dog is running

Here is a fish

Our cat is black

My blue car